STEPHEN BIESTY'S
CROSS-SECTIONS
CASTLE

DK PUBLISHING

LONDON, NEW YORK, MELBOURNE, MUNICH, AND DELHI

Senior Editor Carron Brown
Senior Designer Jim Green

Managing Editor Linda Esposito
Managing Art Editor Diane Peyton Jones

Category Publisher Laura Buller
DK picture librarian Romaine Werblow

Production Controller Gemma Sharpe
Production Editor Francesca Wardell

Jacket Editor Manisha Majithia
Jacket Designer Laura Brim

Publishing Director Jonathan Metcalf
Associate Publishing Director Liz Wheeler
Art Director Phil Ormerod

Consultant Lise Hull

First American Edition, 2013

Published in the United States by
DK Publishing
375 Hudson Street
New York, New York 10014

13 14 15 16 17 10 9 8 7 6 5 4 3 2 1
001—185353—5/13

A catalog record for this book is available from the Library of Congress.

ISBN 978-1-4654-0880-8

DK books are available at special discounts when purchased in bulk for sales promotions,
premiums, fund-raising, or educational use. For details, contact: DK Publishing Special
Markets, 375 Hudson Street, New York, New York 10014 or SpecialSales@dk.com.

Printed and bound in China by Leo.

Discover more at
www.dk.com

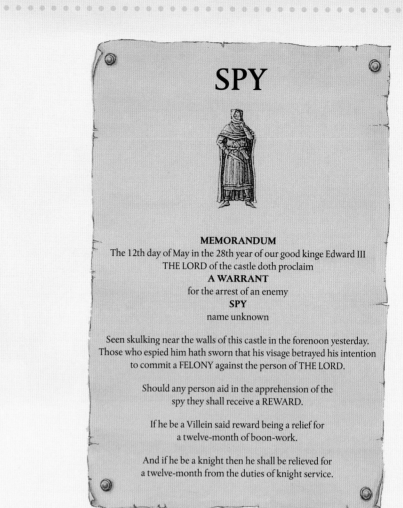

SPY

MEMORANDUM
The 12th day of May in the 28th year of our good kinge Edward III
THE LORD of the castle doth proclaim
A WARRANT
for the arrest of an enemy
SPY
name unknown

Seen skulking near the walls of this castle in the forenoon yesterday.
Those who espied him hath sworn that his visage betrayed his intention
to commit a FELONY against the person of THE LORD.

Should any person aid in the apprehension of the
spy they shall receive a REWARD.

If he be a Villein said reward being a relief for
a twelve-month of boon-work.

And if he be a knight then he shall be relieved for
a twelve-month from the duties of knight service.

STEPHEN BIESTY'S
CROSS-SECTIONS
CASTLE

ILLUSTRATED BY
STEPHEN BIESTY

WRITTEN BY
RICHARD PLATT

Contents

Parts of a castle

Towering high above the landscape, European castles still look commanding. Imagine, then, how powerful a castle appeared 650 years ago when it was new. Bright flags flapped from the towers. Sunlight glinted from the armor of soldiers patrolling the walls. A castle was built to impress. It was the fortified home of a powerful warlord, and from its safety he ruled the surrounding land.

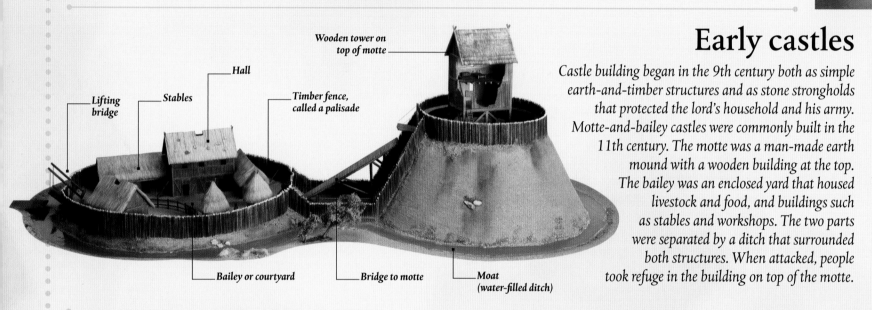

Wooden tower on top of motte

Hall

Stables

Lifting bridge

Timber fence, called a palisade

Bailey or courtyard

Bridge to motte

Moat (water-filled ditch)

Early castles

Castle building began in the 9th century both as simple earth-and-timber structures and as stone strongholds that protected the lord's household and his army. Motte-and-bailey castles were commonly built in the 11th century. The motte was a man-made earth mound with a wooden building at the top. The bailey was an enclosed yard that housed livestock and food, and buildings such as stables and workshops. The two parts were separated by a ditch that surrounded both structures. When attacked, people took refuge in the building on top of the motte.

Stone strongholds

Castles became stronger as methods of warfare changed. There was no standard shape and structure for a castle, but stone rather than wood was used. The builders adapted their designs to suit the site, the budget, and the military dangers of the day.

Meet the castle
The castle in this book dates from about 1350 and is based on Chinon in France, and on Chepstow, which guards the border between England and Wales.

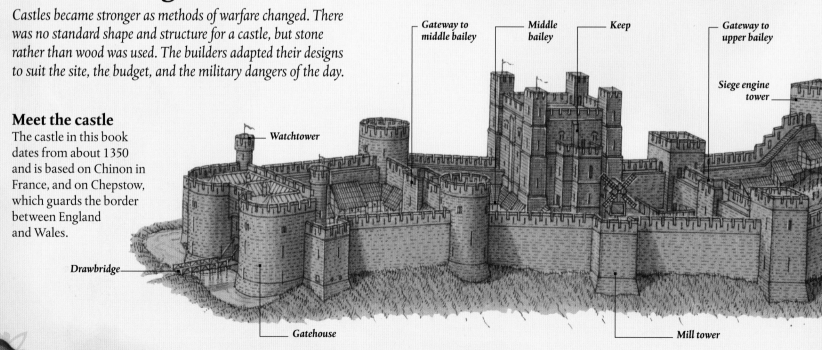

Gateway to middle bailey

Middle bailey

Keep

Gateway to upper bailey

Siege engine tower

Watchtower

Drawbridge

Gatehouse

Mill tower

Watchtower

Back gate

Moat—10 ft (3 m) deep

Hall window

Outer defenses

High walls and strong towers were the castle's main defenses. They kept out attacking soldiers, and the parapets (the walls' jagged tops) provided the defenders with a safe, clear view over the surrounding land. Every castle made use of the natural features of its site. By building the castle on a high point, attackers below faced a devastating shower of arrows from the walls.

Surrounded

The moat was a water-filled ditch enclosing the castle where natural features did not protect it. Bodiam Castle in England has a moat so wide that siege engines and miners would have been useless against it.

Strong features

A high wall surrounded the castle. Defenders manned towers along the walls.

A sturdy gatehouse protected the way into the castle.

The wall enclosed several courtyards, each called a bailey.

If the walls were breached, the defenders retreated to the keep and fought to the death.

Arsenal tower (for storing weapons)

Castle personalities

The noble family lived at the heart of the castle, in the keep or private tower. Everyone else served or protected them. The page was a young servant, but like the knights who fought for the lord, he also came from a noble family. A humble priest led the family's worship and acted as secretary. The fool entertained them, and a host of other workers, such as the gong farmer, kept life in the castle comfortable—or at least bearable.

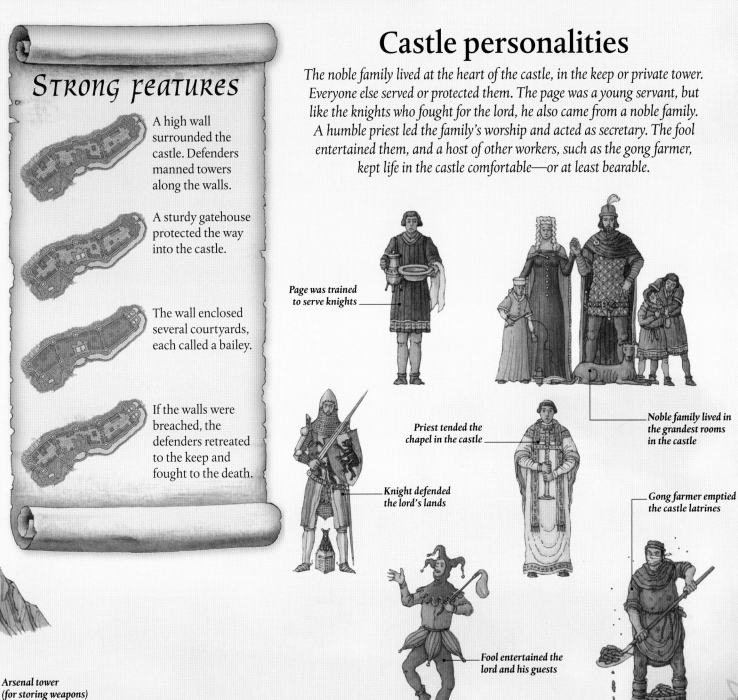

Page was trained to serve knights

Knight defended the lord's lands

Priest tended the chapel in the castle

Noble family lived in the grandest rooms in the castle

Gong farmer emptied the castle latrines

Fool entertained the lord and his guests

The castle gate

Portcullis

The first point of attack was usually the main entrance—the gatehouse. Watchmen perched in the high turrets surveyed the surrounding land through the crenels (gaps in the wall), looking for any movement that would betray the enemy's approach. At the first sign of trouble, the castle sprung into action, gathering supplies, building defenses, and calling the lord's people to the safety of the castle walls. In the unfortunate, and unlikely, event that the enemy ever reached the gate, fiendish and fatal traps awaited the intruder, just inside the entrance.

❶ Latrines
This part of the lower gatehouse tower contained some of the castle's toilets.

The way is barred
Lowering a strong oak grille, called a portcullis, protected the gate against attack. A layer of beaten iron covered the portcullis as a fire precaution.

❷ Thick walls
The thickness of castle walls made them very strong. Most were more than 8 ft (2.5 m) thick, and the walls of the towers were thicker still.

You are here

The gatehouse was the main entrance. It had fortified doors and a drawbridge that could be raised to seal the castle from enemies.

Supplies are brought into the castle

3 Watchmen

Watchmen were among the worst paid garrison members. They earned about the same as farm laborers, and received only one-fifth the pay of skilled workers such as crossbow makers.

4 Crenels

The gaps between the raised sections of stonework were called crenels. The raised sections were called merlons. Embrasures were arrow loops (slits) built into the merlons.

5 Roofing

Attacking armies fired flaming arrows over the walls to set fire to thatched roofs inside, so castle roofs were built from fireproof materials when possible. Lead, tile, or slate worked best.

6 Watch turret

A high tower raised above the castle walls gave a fine view over the nearby countryside. Some castles, such as Urquhart in Scotland, were sited specifically to provide the best possible view.

7 Hoardings

The most important preparation for battle was to build hoardings. These were wooden extensions to the wall-walk, which protected the defenders.

8 Fine leather binding

Animal hides stretched over the hoarding's wooden roof provided some protection from flaming arrows.

9 Drawbridge

In its normal position, the drawbridge or turning bridge spanned the water-filled moat. When danger threatened, the castle guard raised the bridge.

Deep, water-filled moat protects the castle when the drawbridge is raised

Knight giving orders

Gateway guard

Preparing for attack

Surprise attacks on castles were unusual. More often, the castle defenders had plenty of advance warning. While they waited for the enemy to arrive, they were busy preparing and strengthening the castle's defenses. The moat was cleared of as much debris as possible, and the sides of the moat were made steeper to provide a greater obstacle to the attacking hordes.

Church ceiling decoration of a knight on horseback

Summoning knights

The lord summoned loyal knights for guard duty. They were given the task of gathering supplies from the lord's lands to feed the castle inhabitants (both people and animals) and arm the garrison during the siege. While the siege was in full force, the lord's knights would sometimes ride out of the castle to engage in short battles with the enemy's knights. The aim of these battles was to kill or capture as many enemy knights as possible. Captured knights could be ransomed back to the enemy.

Gathering supplies

A castle under attack had to survive on its stockpiles of food and other supplies. The enemy surrounding the castle cut off all supply routes, hoping to force the castle to surrender due to starvation. Before fighting started, the castle guards collected all they could. This often left the peasants in the countryside with nothing to eat.

All kinds of food was gathered and stored in the castle

Wood piles were burned if they couldn't be taken to the castle

Food
Inside the castle, meat and fish were salted, fruit was dried, and sacks of grain were stored to make flour for bread. The castle well provided fresh water and fish, and water birds were caught from the moat.

Leave nothing useful
The enemy ran out of supplies, too. Anything that couldn't be brought to the castle and that the enemy might use, such as livestock, orchards, crops, and houses, was destroyed.

Strengthening defenses

Within the castle's sturdy walls there were ingenious gates and deadly traps. In times of tension, soldiers extended and protected the wall-walk and towers with a wooden corridor called a hoarding. Weapons to be used against the enemy were stockpiled within the castle.

Yoo-hoo!

"Murder holes" in the gateway provided a handy way of shouting orders, but this was not their main function. If the enemy soldiers got through the outer door, the garrison dropped the portcullis and archers then picked them off one by one.

Murder hole

Crossbow bolts

The arrows of crossbows were called quarrels or bolts. The garrison stored them in barrels ready for immediate use. A shower of arrows killed many attackers—quarrels could pierce armor.

Metal bolt tip would have been placed on a wooden shaft

Constructing hoardings

Each timber support was fitted into a hole in the wall, called a putlog hole.

Wooden planks ran between the supports, and upright timbers were fixed to the ends.

Planks formed a wall between the upright timbers, and a sloped roof was put in place.

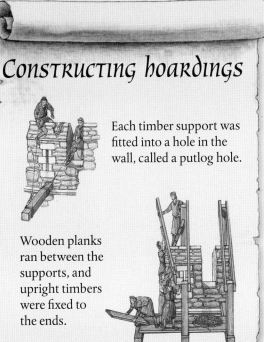

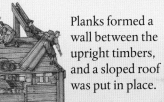

The waiting game

When hostile armies surrounded the castle, soldiers raised the drawbridge and prepared for a furious fight. Inside the castle, the garrison waited for reinforcements or hoped that the attackers would go away. The besieging army waited for the inhabitants to die of hunger or disease.

Signaling a siege

A siege formally began only when the attacking forces fired their siege weapons, such as trebuchets, against the castle walls. Until this signal, the commander could surrender his castle and its inhabitants without shame.

The simplest trebuchets had no counterweight. Instead, troops just pulled down on the shorter end of the arm

Sling

Pivoting arm

Shelter and survival

Women and children took shelter in the castle when fighting began. But if food ran out, anyone who couldn't fight was ejected. The attackers would not let them pass, so many starved to death. The survivors ate anything they could find, including dogs and rats.

TREBUCHET

Under siege

In peacetime, the castle could be an office, a home, a storehouse, and even a market. But in wartime, the castle threw off these peaceful guises. It became a fortress, in control of a wide area. When hostile armies surrounded the castle, soldiers raised the drawbridge and prepared for battle. A siege had begun! Long hours were spent trying to break into the castle. Often the attackers bribed someone inside to open the gates, or they waited for the inhabitants to die of hunger or disease. Sometimes, the siege ended because attackers and defenders made a formal agreement, much like a modern peace treaty.

You are here

If the enemy managed to reach the gatehouse, the garrison swarmed to its defense. Water was stored in case of fire, and archers fired from arrow loops.

❶ Trebuchet
The trebuchet was a large siege engine that hurled projectiles high in the air—over the castle walls—up to a distance of 980 ft (300 m).

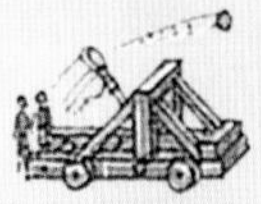

❷ Mangonel
The mangonel threw projectiles on a low trajectory (they did not fly high in the sky). Rocks smashed against the castle, rather than flying over the wall into the bailey.

Counterweight swings arm over to release the missile

Archers firing incendiary arrows

Pulley

Catapulting severed heads

Soldiers called sappers mining under the walls to make them collapse

❸ Bats in the belfry

The biggest siege engine, the belfry, was a wooden tower that held hundreds of men. Lowering the drawbridge allowed these men to swarm across into the castle.

❹ Pull up the ladder

Only desperate or foolish soldiers tried to scale the walls on ladders, because they were defenseless as they climbed the swaying poles.

❺ Cats, rats, and tortoises

Soldiers at the wall worked under a wheeled shelter. They moved it forward slowly, and so the shelter got the nickname "tortoise." It was also called a "cat" or a "rat" because of its creeping advance.

❻ Rolling road

Soldiers in the cat tried to fill the moat with rocks and soil. Then they built a roadway of logs to form a bridge to the castle walls.

❼ A nice blaze

Flaming arrows could ignite the whole wooden hoarding, so later castles used machicolation instead. This was an overhanging stone extension to the wall-walk.

❽ Murderous missiles

Soldiers catapulted pots of lime that burned the skin, or dead animals that might introduce disease into the castle. For a really grisly attack, besiegers fired severed human heads.

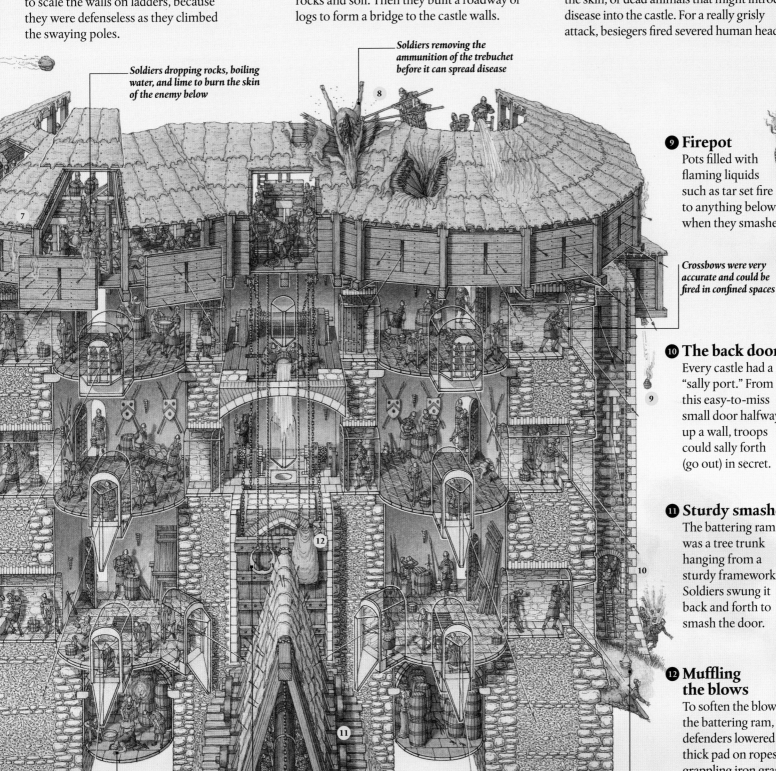

Soldiers dropping rocks, boiling water, and lime to burn the skin of the enemy below

Soldiers removing the ammunition of the trebuchet before it can spread disease

❾ Firepot

Pots filled with flaming liquids such as tar set fire to anything below when they smashed.

Crossbows were very accurate and could be fired in confined spaces

❿ The back door

Every castle had a "sally port." From this easy-to-miss small door halfway up a wall, troops could sally forth (go out) in secret.

⓫ Sturdy smasher

The battering ram was a tree trunk hanging from a sturdy framework. Soldiers swung it back and forth to smash the door.

⓬ Muffling the blows

To soften the blows of the battering ram, the defenders lowered a thick pad on ropes. A grappling iron grasped the ram and stopped it from swinging.

Vibrations caused by mining make ripples in a bowl of water

Grappling iron

Attacking soldiers using a battering ram on the castle gate

Pots of burning sulfur smoking out sappers

Locked up

The group of soldiers guarding the castle was called the garrison. They spent much of their time in the gatehouse that controlled the entrance. Only the most determined invasion force could enter the castle once the garrison had secured their stronghold. The gatehouse also served as the castle prison. Nobles captured in battle had luxury quarters in one of the towers. They were held until their family paid a ransom (a large fee), although few prisoners were this lucky.

Could be worse

The life of a ransom prisoner was really quite good. He may even have had the freedom to roam the castle if he gave his word not to escape. Some prisoners signed a document upon surrendering, in which they agreed to be obedient prisoners.

❶ A slippery climb

Invaders even tried climbing up the latrine shaft to get in the castle. This approach broke the siege of Château Gaillard, France, in 1204. However, if the invaders got stuck and died, the drains needed a good cleaning before the latrine could be used again.

❷ Treasure chest

The constable guarded the valuables of the castle and was probably quite wealthy himself. His job was usually well-paid and provided many extra opportunities to get rich.

You are here

The massive gatehouse towers kept prisoners in as effectively as they kept invaders out. Every dark nook was put to use as a room for criminals or guards.

Retrieving the dead after a battle

❸ Lookout

Nicknamed "Jim Crow" because of his lofty perch, the lookout sounded a series of coded calls on his hunting horn to signal the approach of friends or enemies.

❹ Winch room

The portcullis that protected the gateway was very heavy. The garrison used a winch so that two men could lift it between them. Lowering the portcullis was easy: Knocking out a stop or brake let it drop quickly to trap intruders.

❺ Constable's quarters

The most luxurious gatehouse room was the constable's. This important man controlled the castle when the lord and his family were away. He was responsible for every aspect of the day-to-day routine: for authorizing spending on building and repairs, for supplying provisions, and for the security of prisoners.

❻ Peepholes

Holes in the entrance arch allowed guards in side passages to inspect visitors in safety.

❼ Gates within gates

Even in peacetime, the castle gates were shut at night. Visitors entered through a wicket gate—a small door within the main gate.

❽ Forget-me-not

Hidden at the back of the dungeon was a cramped cell-within-a-cell. This "oubliette" took its name from the French word *oublier*, to forget. Unwanted prisoners were pushed into the oubliette and forgotten.

❾ Squint

A tiny peephole called a squint allowed the jailer to check on his charges.

❿ Smelly job

Emptying the latrine pit was an unpleasant and unhealthy task. The unfortunate worker with the bucket and shovel was called a "gong farmer."

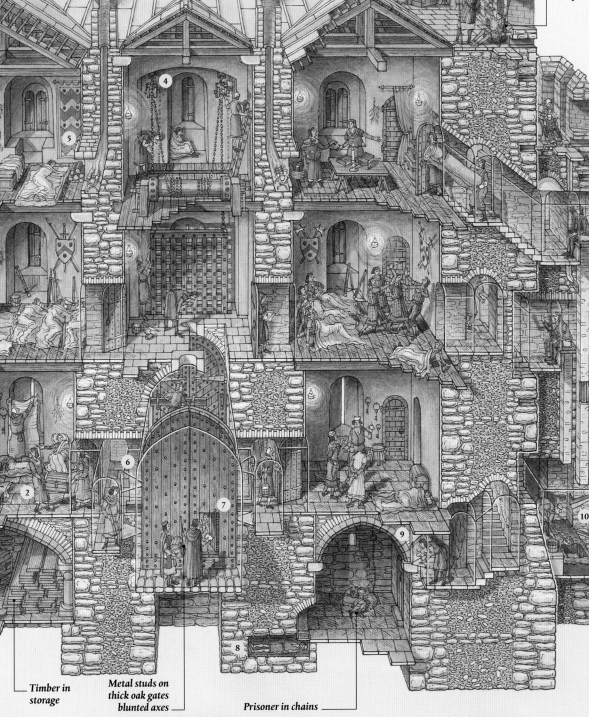

Guard caught asleep on watch

Timber in storage

Metal studs on thick oak gates blunted axes

Prisoner in chains

The feudal system

The lord of the castle (usually a wealthy knight or baron) did not own the land in the sense that we understand today. The lord earned the right to build a castle and use land by swearing an oath of loyalty to a baron or to the king. The lord promised to do knight service (to fight on horseback) if the king needed help in war.

Who's who?

Many people who lived on the land were under the lord's control. The lord protected them, in exchange for fines or fees. This social structure was called feudalism. By the 14th century, feudalism had evolved. Instead of knight service, the lord paid money to the king or baron, who used it to hire soldiers when he needed them. This system was called bastard feudalism.

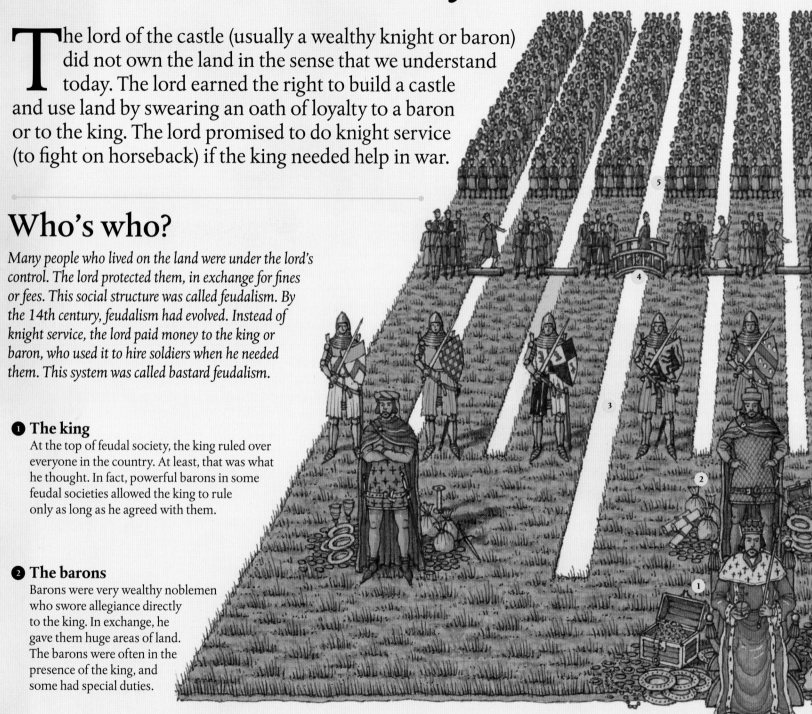

❶ The king
At the top of feudal society, the king ruled over everyone in the country. At least, that was what he thought. In fact, powerful barons in some feudal societies allowed the king to rule only as long as he agreed with them.

❷ The barons
Barons were very wealthy noblemen who swore allegiance directly to the king. In exchange, he gave them huge areas of land. The barons were often in the presence of the king, and some had special duties.

❸ The knights
Barons could not control all their land without help, so they in turn divided it between rich knights. Each knight swore allegiance to a baron, and owed him 40 days' knight service a year.

❹ Freemen
A few of the people on the castle lands were freemen. They had a slightly higher status than villeins (see right), and were free to move to another manor.

❺ Villeins, or peasants
The lord protected the people on his land in exchange for money, goods such as farm produce, or work. Most people were villeins: little better than slaves. They could not leave the lord's lands.

The license

Wax seal with the lord's image made the document official

The king's secretary or scribe wrote out the license on a sheet of parchment.

The license to crenellate was awarded to a lord by the king.

Licence to crenellate

Building a castle needed royal permission. This was called "licence to crenellate," because it was the crenellations (battlements) that made a castle different from all other buildings. Adulterine castles (illegally fortified houses) could be seized by the king.

Crenellations

JAMILLE CASTLE, SPAIN
(15TH CENTURY)

Canvas gear bag with bowls

Glaive—a pole weapon for knocking or stabbing

Belt bag containing personal belongings

Helmet

GUARD'S POSSESSIONS

Chain splints kept swords from slicing through arm

Quilted jacket made from layered canvas

Metal gauntlet protected hand

Guard duty

A wealthy man who farmed the lord's land paid rent by contributing to the castle guard. He had to provide soldiers, weapons, armor, and sometimes horses. These duties resulted from the act of homage, when the man put his hands between those of his lord and swore to "be his man." "Paying homage" still means performing duties for a more important person, or promising to.

Castle building

Only a rich and powerful lord could afford to build a castle. He chose a position with solid foundations to take the huge weight and a site that was important to hold in a battle. The castle was also an administrative center and usually had to be within a day's walk of the lord's lands, with ample supplies of food and fuel within easy reach. Finally, within the castle walls there needed to be a source of clean drinking water to supply the defenders and livestock during a siege.

Metal and wood

Anything made from metal was costly because making iron required huge amounts of fuel. For a blacksmith to make 55 lb (25 kg) of iron required one mature oak tree. Trees were also needed as building materials themselves. They were made into lighter beams by sawyers (workers who sawed wood) to build wooden structures in the castle.

Carpenter's hammer

Stonemason's chisel

Making holes

A carpenter made holes with an auger or awl. After a few turns, he pulled it from the hole to remove chippings. Drill bits, which have a spiral groove to remove wood chips continuously, did not appear until the 15th century.

Awl

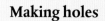

Chisel

Billhook was used as a cutting tool

Tools and nails

Tradesmen made many of their own tools or had them made locally by the blacksmith. Shapes of tools varied from place to place: There were no standard designs. An important part of the blacksmith's work was making nails from hammered lengths of wire.

Adze (like an ax, but with the blade turned to cross the handle)

Broadax

The walls

Some interior buildings were made from wood, but most of the castle was built from stone. But not all stone was suitable for castle walls. Very hard stone, such as granite, was difficult to cut. The most suitable stone was called freestone. The masons trimmed it into ashlar: regular flat-surfaced blocks, and the shapes needed for the arrow loops and arches.

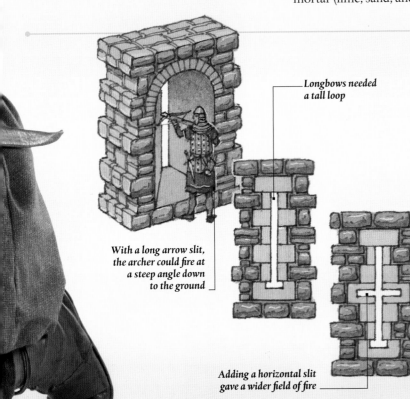

Daub   Wattle

Wattle and daub

To fill the gaps between wooden beams, builders wove wattle (panels of hazel twigs) and plastered them with daub (a mixture of clay, animal dung, and horsehair) to make them waterproof.

Stone walls

Neatly trimmed blocks of ashlar formed the outer and inner wall surfaces. Between them was a filling of rubble: stones of assorted size held together with mortar (lime, sand, and water).

Ashlar
Rubble
Ashlar

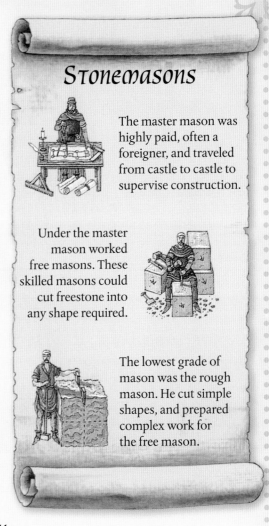

Stonemasons

The master mason was highly paid, often a foreigner, and traveled from castle to castle to supervise construction.

Under the master mason worked free masons. These skilled masons could cut freestone into any shape required.

The lowest grade of mason was the rough mason. He cut simple shapes, and prepared complex work for the free mason.

Arrow loops

Archers fired through narrow slits, called arrow loops, in the castle wall. Arrow loops were splayed (spread out) on the inside so that an archer could take careful aim without exposing himself to fire. Not all slits in the wall were for firing arrows. Many were used in place of windows, letting in air and light.

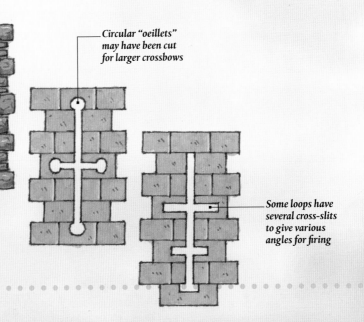

Longbows needed a tall loop

With a long arrow slit, the archer could fire at a steep angle down to the ground

Adding a horizontal slit gave a wider field of fire

Circular "oeillets" may have been cut for larger crossbows

Some loops have several cross-slits to give various angles for firing

Repairs

During and after the siege, the castle needed repairs. Its walls, battlements, and roofs suffered most of the damage from siege engines. Burned timbers, thatch, and crushed stonework were replaced. When they weren't fighting, the men of the garrison became strong hands to help with rebuilding work. The weather also caused problems, such as rotting timber, and the castle was constantly being repaired. All this, of course, used up time and money.

Early recycling
Lead was too precious to waste. The roofers melted down old lead and made new sheets by pouring the molten metal onto a flat bed of sand.

You are here

The lower bailey provided refuge to villeins in time of siege. In peacetime, craftspeople lived and worked here. A large building housed the castle court.

❶ Heavy load
Much of the stone for the castle had to come from a quarry nearby. Transporting it by cart over even a short distance doubled its cost.

❷ Basket boys
Mortar and smaller stones went up the walls in baskets carried on laborers' shoulders.

❸ Scaffolding
In order to work on the walls as they grew higher, the craftsmen built scaffolding. Holes in the walls, called putlog holes, supported the inner ends of some of the timbers.

Stone blocks

Stonemason's work area

Wattle-and-daub walls sealed with lime

Master mason

Mason carving blocks

Making mortar— a mixture of lime, sand, and water

❹ Lifting gear
This simple crane was fixed, but more elaborate types, called skewing cranes, rotated to bring the load directly over the rising tower.

❺ Treadmill
Two men walked around inside the wheel to turn it and raise up the load, much as a hamster runs in an exercise wheel.

❻ Thatcher at work
The cheapest roofing material was thatch. This was a thick covering of reeds, straw, heather, or even bracken.

❼ Making bate
Tannery workers softened animal skins by soaking them in bate—water mixed with dog excrement. A barefoot workman trampled the bate to a pulp in a vat.

Lead sheeting

❽ Shingles
By splitting oak logs into thin, flat rectangles called shingles, woodsmen made a cheap, lightweight roofing material. However, shingles rotted quickly and the nails securing them rusted.

❾ Blazing roof
Thatch was the cheapest roofing material but it burned easily. Attacking forces fired flaming arrows to ignite the thatch or fired burning barrels of tar from a trebuchet.

❿ Here comes the judge
The lord himself was the judge of serious crimes, but for lesser cases, an official such as the steward might take his place. A jury of 12 men listened to evidence and decided guilt or innocence in serious cases.

⓫ Taxes
When the people of the manor came to pay the lord what they owed, a lesser official checked the payments. A scribe noted the payment in the castle records, which were written by hand on parchment (hammered animal skins).

⓬ Court archive
The castle cellar housed court documents. They were called the rolls, because the clerk recorded everything on sheets of parchment that were rolled for storage.

⓭ Well, well!
A reliable supply of water was essential for the castle to survive a siege.

Blacksmith

Hard at work

Every day, the bailey rang with the shouts and curses of busy craft workers whose workshops clustered around its wall. "You stupid apprentice! Have you got ale froth for brains? Give me that hammer!" When things went wrong (which was quite often), it was usually the youngest apprentice, or trainee worker, who got the blame. Most manufacturing and processing took place in the castle or nearby. Billowing steam swirled round the wheelwrights fitting a metal rim to a cartwheel. Deafening hammering from the armorer almost drowned out the sound of the wind in the mill sails.

Moving up the ladder

An apprentice lived with a master craftsman and paid a large sum of money to learn his craft, which generally took seven years. The apprentice then became a journeyman and was paid a wage. One day, he would become a master craftsman.

❶ Clearing the ditch

Workers used baskets to carry the rich mud they dug out from the ditch. They fertilized the nearby fields with the mud.

❷ Cutting brushwood

The willow saplings growing in the ditch didn't go to waste. Farm animals browsed on the leaves, and the hurdle-maker used the branches to make gates and fences.

❸ Plumber

The plumber shaped and joined lead sheets and pipes, and his trade took its name from the Latin word for lead, *plumbum*.

Painting the walls with limewash

Polishing armor to remove rust

Chain mail being made

Official checking progress

You are here

In a siege, the keep was the last place of refuge, so it was designed to be defended easily. A drawbridge and steep stairs sometimes guarded the entrance.

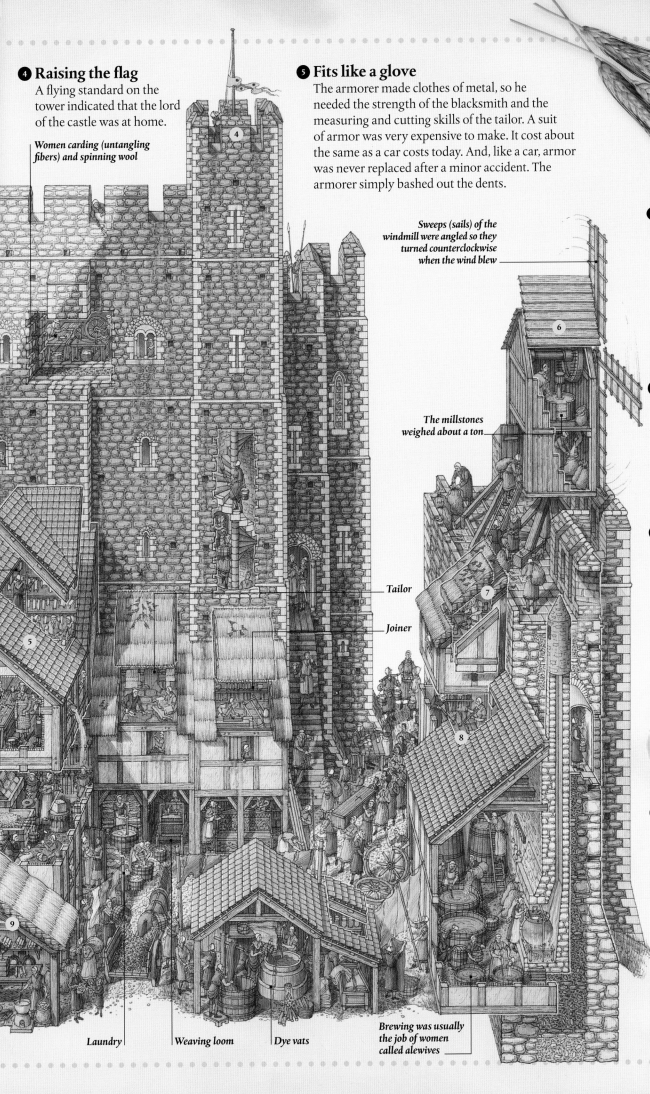

4 Raising the flag
A flying standard on the tower indicated that the lord of the castle was at home.

Women carding (untangling fibers) and spinning wool

5 Fits like a glove
The armorer made clothes of metal, so he needed the strength of the blacksmith and the measuring and cutting skills of the tailor. A suit of armor was very expensive to make. It cost about the same as a car costs today. And, like a car, armor was never replaced after a minor accident. The armorer simply bashed out the dents.

Sweeps (sails) of the windmill were angled so they turned counterclockwise when the wind blew

The millstones weighed about a ton

Tailor

Joiner

6 Multure
Everyone had to have their corn ground at the lord's mill. The lord charged a fee, called multure, for this service. It was usually between $1/16$ and $1/24$ of the flour, or the equivalent in money.

7 Throwing pots
The potter made round bowls, jars, and plates using a turntable. He threw the clay onto the turntable, so the process of making pots was called throwing.

8 Atilliator
The crossbow maker, or atilliator, was the most skilled of craftsmen, and was paid 50 percent more than other workers.

9 More candles!
Candles were an important source of artificial light, and the chandler (candlemaker) was kept very busy when the lord was in residence. A grand household could burn 100 lb (45 kg) of wax and tallow in a single winter's night—the equivalent of 1,300 candles.

Laundry *Weaving loom* *Dye vats*

Brewing was usually the job of women called alewives

27

Clothing

In medieval times, clothing was important for advertising your status if you were wealthy. Silk, worn by nobles, was the most expensive fabric, since it came all the way from China. There were laws in some places that prevented those of a lower standing from wearing fine textiles. For example, an apprentice would not be allowed to wear clothes like those of his master craftsman.

Pushing the wheel made the distaff turn

Fleece is pulled into a thread by hand

Distaff

Preparing the threads

No matter if people were rich or poor, all clothing was made from natural sources—animals, plants, and insects. There were clothes of linen, leather, silk, cotton, and fur, but the most widely available fiber was wool. More material meant more cost so garments were generally simple unless it was a noble's outfit.

Spinning
This new invention was the first laborsaving machine to use a continuous turning motion and a belt drive. Until the early 14th century, women spun yarn by twisting it onto a distaff—a long pole.

Washing fleeces
Wool from a sheep's back is very greasy and dirty. Pegging the fleece to wash it in a stream helped clean it, but scrubbing it in urine diluted with water was a more effective way of degreasing.

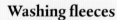

Fleece

Weld leaves and woad (a European herb) made a green dye

Woad created a blue dye

Dyeing
To set a color, the dyer boiled the yarn or fabric in a huge vat, turning the material constantly to get an even shade. Different plant ingredients created a variety of colors.

Weld leaves created a yellow dye

Oak bark made a brown dye

Madder roots made orange and red dyes

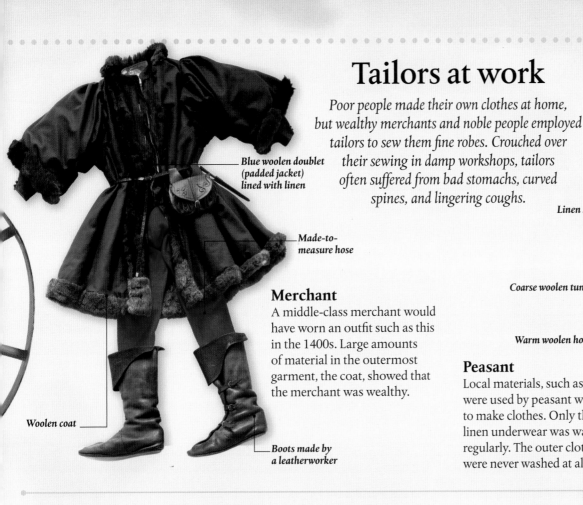

Tailors at work

Poor people made their own clothes at home, but wealthy merchants and noble people employed tailors to sew them fine robes. Crouched over their sewing in damp workshops, tailors often suffered from bad stomachs, curved spines, and lingering coughs.

Blue woolen doublet (padded jacket) lined with linen

Made-to-measure hose

Merchant

A middle-class merchant would have worn an outfit such as this in the 1400s. Large amounts of material in the outermost garment, the coat, showed that the merchant was wealthy.

Woolen coat

Boots made by a leatherworker

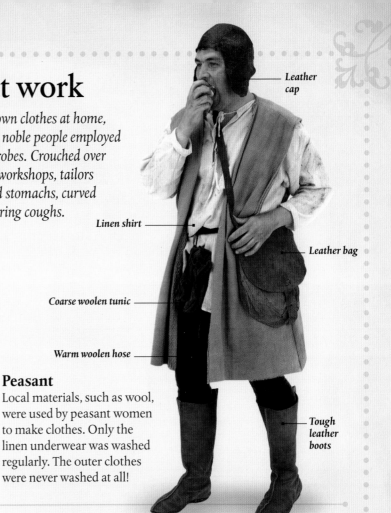

Leather cap

Linen shirt

Leather bag

Coarse woolen tunic

Warm woolen hose

Peasant

Local materials, such as wool, were used by peasant women to make clothes. Only the linen underwear was washed regularly. The outer clothes were never washed at all!

Tough leather boots

Dressing for battle

Armor changed and evolved constantly. In the 14th century, knights wore three layers of body armor over their shirts and hose. The innermost layer, a quilted knee-length coat or aketon, was all that poor foot soldiers could afford. On top of this knights wore chain mail, then a "coat of plates," overlapping panels of metal riveted to a sturdy shirt. Finally, the surcoat kept the sun off the armor.

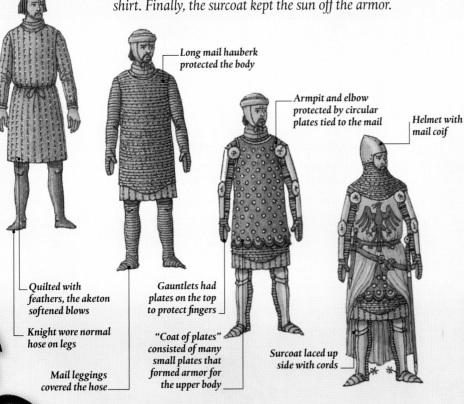

Long mail hauberk protected the body

Armpit and elbow protected by circular plates tied to the mail

Helmet with mail coif

Quilted with feathers, the aketon softened blows

Knight wore normal hose on legs

Mail leggings covered the hose

Gauntlets had plates on the top to protect fingers

"Coat of plates" consisted of many small plates that formed armor for the upper body

Surcoat laced up side with cords

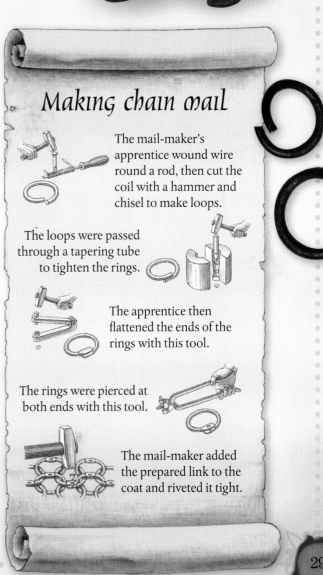

Making chain mail

The mail-maker's apprentice wound wire round a rod, then cut the coil with a hammer and chisel to make loops.

The loops were passed through a tapering tube to tighten the rings.

The apprentice then flattened the ends of the rings with this tool.

The rings were pierced at both ends with this tool.

The mail-maker added the prepared link to the coat and riveted it tight.

LIVING LIKE A LORD

The lord of the castle and his family lived in grand style. The greatest luxury, though, was privacy. They had suites of rooms such as the solar, a kind of studio attached to the great hall where they could withdraw from their servants and guests and do as they pleased. For everyone else, privacy was impossible. All poor people lived their lives in full view of their neighbors, friends, and family.

Pricey glass
Glass of any kind was hugely expensive, and the chapel was often the only part of the castle with glass windows. Other castle windows were covered by oak shutters.

❶ Target practice
The quintain was a device for knights to practice the joust. Originally a shield fixed to a post, it evolved into a pivoted structure with a counterweight that could knock the rider from his horse.

❷ Gallery
In the thick wall of the tower, a gallery provided access to other rooms and staircases. Musicians also played from the gallery during feasts.

❸ The largest room
The great hall served many purposes. In early castles, almost all activity took place there. The lord and his family ate and even slept there. Later, the lord used it for business and for formal meals.

❹ Sleep tight
After his horses and armor, a lord's bed was usually his most prized possession. It was certainly the most valuable piece of furniture in the castle.

❺ Bloodletting
The cure for almost any disease was bloodletting. The physician cut open a vein in the patient's arm and let blood drain out of it. However, death often followed quickly.

You are here

The lord and his family lived in the keep at the center of the castle. Important people such as the physician and chaplain also lived here, and worked for the lord.

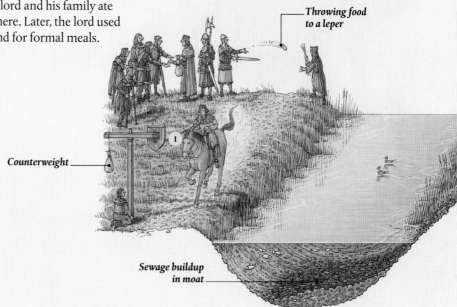

Throwing food to a leper

Counterweight

Sewage buildup in moat

❻ Treasury
Every castle of any size had a strong room for storing money. The lord collected taxes for the king, and he had to store this money as well as his own.

❼ Chapel
Worship played an important part in castle life, so the chapel was conveniently close to the domestic rooms. The chapel was traditionally the highest room, with nothing between it and heaven.

Solar

Chaplain's room

Vaulted chapel ceiling was made of arches of stone

Betrothal ceremony

School

Cats control rats and mice

Archive

Torture chamber

❾ Water levels
By creating a well shaft in the wall, it was possible to draw water up several floors.

❽ A pinch of pepper
Petty thieving was common, since spices were far too expensive for ordinary people to afford. An ounce of pepper, for example, could cost a laborer as much as a week's pay.

Noble family

T he lord lived in the castle with his wife (the lady of the manor) and their children. The family's status in society depended on spending money and appearing to enjoy life. And spend they did: on lavish food, on richly embroidered wall hangings, on beautiful clothes, on gold and silver plates, and on entertaining friends and relations. Luckily, to help with this lifestyle, they had personal servants and skilled workers who, in turn, were in charge of a host of lower-ranking servants.

Lords and ladies of large castles wore expensive clothing, especially during feasts

The lord and lady

Nobody married for love. Instead, aristocratic families arranged for their sons and daughters to marry other children of noble birth. The priest blessed the arrangement in a betrothal ceremony when the children were as young as four, although 11 was more common.

Lady of the manor

When the lord was away, the lady of the manor ran the household. She was in charge of the children and their education, the servants, the kitchen, and the castle menu, although cooking was left to the kitchen staff.

Head of the castle

The castle lord was a knight with a noble title who fought for the king. He was responsible for the castle and its surrounding land and villages. Out of all the people in the castle, usually only the lord had a private room.

Children

The lady of the manor employed nurses to look after very young children. By age seven, boys and girls began their school education. Often, noble children were sent to another lord's castle to learn the ways of the castle court. A son served the lord as a page, then as a squire, then, around the age of 21, as a knight. A daughter learned sewing and embroidery, singing, and the important skill of managing the castle household.

Hat worn by girls to keep their hair clean and tidy

Boy's metal toy sword

Working close to the family

There were many servants in the castle, but only a selection worked closely with the lord's family. The ladies-in-waiting were noblewomen who attended the lady of the manor. Pages and squires were also nobles who performed personal services for the family, such as serving food. A few skilled professionals, such as the chaplain and the doctor, were castle residents who the family could call on when needed.

Personal servant
The lord's servant guarded him at night and often slept in the same room on a small bed. He would also have to make sure the lord was kept warm.

Tapestries were hung on the walls to keep a room's warmth in

Priest
The priest was one of the best-educated people in the castle. He held services in the chapel on Sundays and guided the household on religious matters. He helped with castle administration and with the education of the children.

Doctor
Physicians were respected and wealthy. Cures were a combination of astrology, herbal preparations, change of diet, bloodletting, and prayer, and often did little to help the sick recover.

Sweet-smelling herbs hanging on the walls helped perfume the air

Possessions

Even rich people had few possessions in the sense that we understand today. In a typical lord's 14th-century household, the most expensive items were the robes and hangings for the chapel. Along with household tapestries, these made up half the value of the lord's goods. Beds, clothes, gold, and silver made up the rest.

Scribe left space for decoration

Manuscripts were written on stretched animal skin, or parchment

Books
Until printing became widespread in Europe in the 15th century, scribes copied all books in handwriting. This made books valuable and rare possessions. Many nobles owned only a Bible.

A silver lining
Silver plate (tableware) wasn't just a display for the dinner table. Buying plate was an investment, because the silver could be melted down and sold when times were hard.

Lord's Feast

During festivals, or when the lord had noble guests, it was a time for feasting in the castle. The kitchens worked day and night, and walls echoed with crackling fires and the songs of minstrels. The menus for castle banquets seem odd today. Now, we serve different kinds of food—such as salad, meat, and dessert—in individual courses. But in the 14th century, castle cooks mixed sweet and savory. In a single course, roast heron and a pig's head might share the table with pike and a sickly sweet pie made of cream, eggs, dates, and prunes.

Wine cellar
In mid-14th century England, one gallon of wine imported from France cost the equivalent of a day's wages for a skilled laborer. Wine was sold in barrels holding 120–240 gallons.

Nobleman shaving by rubbing his chin with a pumice stone

Servants dressing nobleman

Roast swan

Sugar castle

❶ Castle stream
The moat was not just for defense. It was a source of fish, and game birds bred on artificial islands. Reeds and rushes on the banks provided thatching materials.

Leftover trenchers (stale bread) being handed out to the poor

Large fish being moved to another pond

You are here
The great hall in the keep was the largest and most important room and the social center of castle life. It was also the perfect place for entertaining.

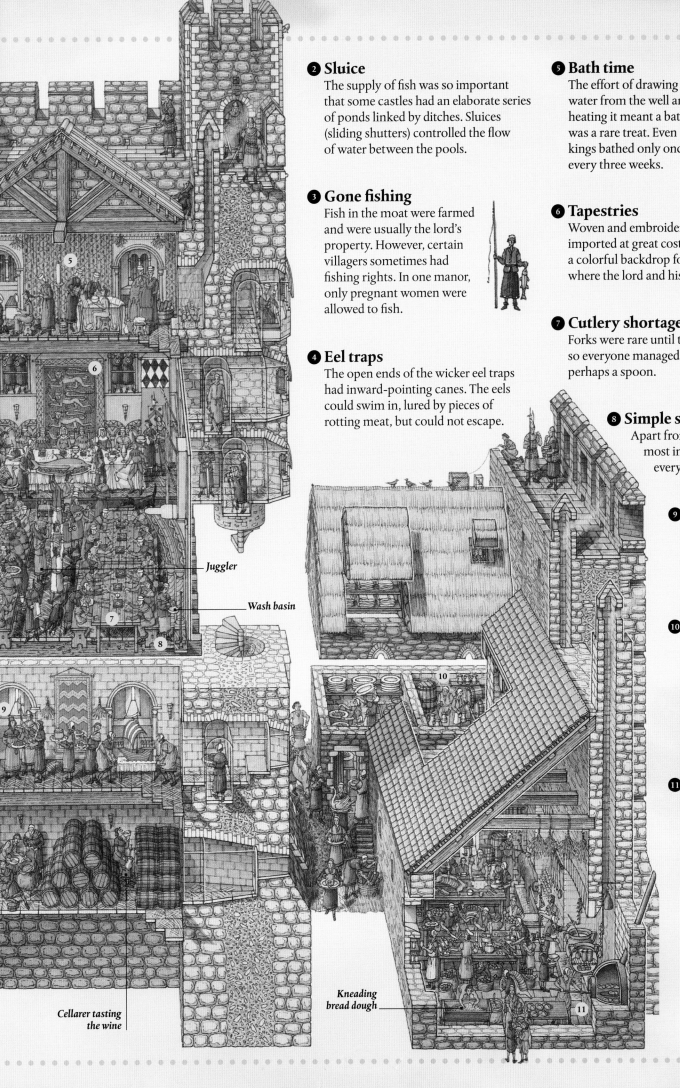

❷ Sluice

The supply of fish was so important that some castles had an elaborate series of ponds linked by ditches. Sluices (sliding shutters) controlled the flow of water between the pools.

❸ Gone fishing

Fish in the moat were farmed and were usually the lord's property. However, certain villagers sometimes had fishing rights. In one manor, only pregnant women were allowed to fish.

❹ Eel traps

The open ends of the wicker eel traps had inward-pointing canes. The eels could swim in, lured by pieces of rotting meat, but could not escape.

❺ Bath time

The effort of drawing water from the well and heating it meant a bath was a rare treat. Even kings bathed only once every three weeks.

❻ Tapestries

Woven and embroidered fabrics were imported at great cost. They formed a colorful backdrop for the top table where the lord and his guests sat.

❼ Cutlery shortage

Forks were rare until the 17th century, so everyone managed with a knife and perhaps a spoon.

❽ Simple seating

Apart from the lord and the most important guests, everyone sat on benches.

❾ Food taster

The castle taster sampled each dish for poison before any royals or nobles ate.

❿ Buttery

Even the smallest castles had a buttery (bottlery). Here, the bottler dispensed the wine. This word has been changed to *butter* today.

⓫ Baker's dozen

Peasants had to bake their bread in the castle oven. They paid the lord in loaves for the use of the oven, and paid a fine if the reeve (village policeman) caught them baking at home.

Juggler

Wash basin

Cellarer tasting the wine

Kneading bread dough

Medieval meals

In medieval times, there were no freezers to keep food fresh, but unless there was a natural disaster or a siege, fresh food was easy to come by. There was meat from wild and domestic animals, grains, vegetables, roots, herbs, spices, fruits, and dairy products. Many familiar foods, such as potatoes and corn from the Americas, had not been discovered by castle dwellers. However, some exotic fruits came to the lord's table via tradesmen from Asia.

Kitchen preparations

Castle kitchens could be huge and consisted of several rooms: One royal castle had enough space to roast three whole oxen. As many as 50 kitchen workers could be employed preparing a feast. There was at least one large hearth for cooking and many tables for grinding herbs, chopping vegetables, and slicing trenchers.

Trencher
Food was not served on plates. Instead, everyone had a trencher—a thick slice of stale bread—on which servants placed food. After the meal, a servant called a ewerer brought water for the lord to wash his fingers.

Faster! Faster!
There were no mechanical aids to cooking, and spit-roasted meat required constant turning. The job of the turnspit was the lowliest in the kitchen. In later centuries, this work was done by a dog, running round inside a wheel.

Not so subtle
To end each course, servants brought in an elaborate dish called a subtlety. This was more a sculpture than food, and was crafted from sugar.

What's on the menu?

There were laws dictating who could eat which foods. The rich ate costly, delicate foods, while the poor had to do with low-cost, readily available meals. However, everyone dreamed of the plentiful, delicious dishes that adorned the tables at a feast.

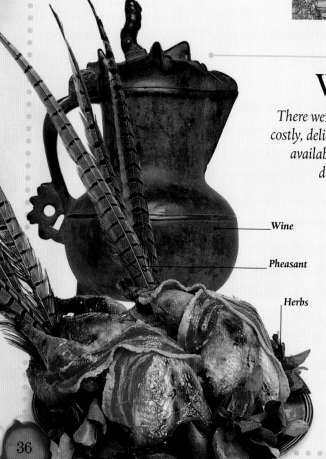

Wine

Pheasant

Herbs

Bacon

Milk

Cheese

Feasting like a lord
Wealthy castle dwellers ate almost anything that moved—and much else. Besides fish, beef, pork, and lamb, a feast might feature birds of every size, from herons to larks. These were baked in pies, or simply roasted.

Eating like a peasant
In contrast to the wealthy, poor people had a simple and boring diet. They ate mainly bread and pottage (thick vegetable soup) with a little bacon, milk, and cheese.

CLOVES

CUMIN

ANISEED

GARLIC

GINGER

Flavoring and seasoning

Spices were very costly, and spiced food was a sign of wealth and luxury. Kitchen cupboards bulged with exotic flavorings. Castle cooks used no salt to season the food. Instead, lucky diners helped themselves from a boat-shaped salt cellar. This was placed in front of the lord, separating him and his family and guests from others at the table. The salt became a measure of social status, and even today, describing someone as "below the salt" means they are not respectable.

CORIANDER

CINNAMON

PEPPER

LICORICE   SALT

Eat and be merry!

Large and sumptuous feasts were held in the great hall, and diners were treated to a fantastic show with jugglers, acrobats, musicians, and jesters. The lord's table was at the top of the room so he could watch the whole feast. This table was the closest to the fireplace—such a large room could be very cold.

Musical meals

In grand castles, music might have accompanied a whole meal, but usually musicians played only between courses. Minstrels sang songs, and troubadours played instruments such as drums, flutes, lutes, fiddles, harps, and bagpipes. The guests may also have sung and danced.

— *Lute*

— *Gemshorn*

Jester

The fool or jester was a privileged entertainer. His colorful outfit made fun of fashionable clothes. Wealthy and powerful people allowed him to tell funny stories or sing rude songs about them.

Table manners

Do not spit upon or over the table.

If there is a man of God (such as a priest) at the table, take special care where you spit.

Do not pick your teeth at the table with a knife, straw, or stick.

Do not belch near anyone's face if you have bad breath.

ENTERTAINMENT

Castle life was sometimes cold, often uncomfortable, but never boring. When the day's work was done, the lord and his family amused themselves with sports, such as hunting and jousting. Hunting took many forms, some of which continue today. The most noble was hawking—sending tame birds of prey to swoop down and capture smaller birds. Hunting with dogs was popular, too. The hawks, dogs, and other hunting animals were highly prized, and they lived a better life than many poor people. Jousting was the most glamorous sport, though.

········ You are here ·······

Between the keep and the gateway to the lower bailey were the castle gardens. Nobles would visit the formal garden for moments of quiet in a pleasant space.

❶ Hawking
Wealthy castle dwellers thought hunting with a bird of prey was the finest of sports. The trained birds lived like kings, perching on their owner's wrist and going with him everywhere— to meals and even church.

❷ Delightfully decorative
Lances could be elaborately decorated. The sound of splintering lances delighted audiences. When one heroic knight got through 300 brightly colored lances in one day, he had to use the unpainted ones.

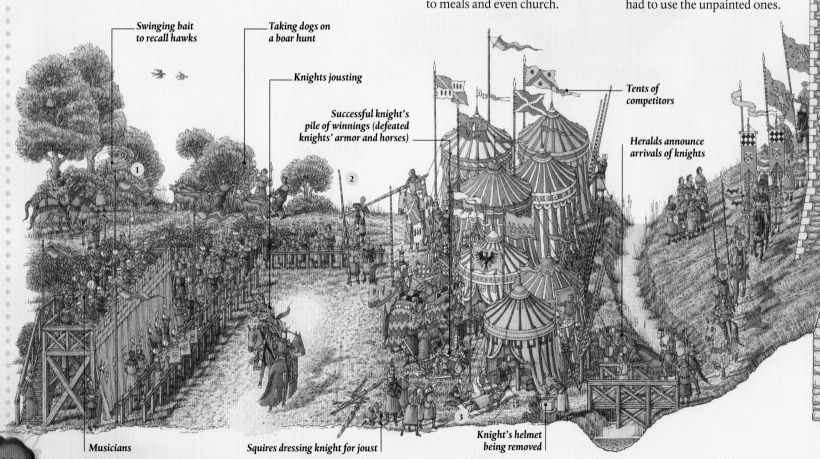

Swinging bait to recall hawks

Taking dogs on a boar hunt

Knights jousting

Successful knight's pile of winnings (defeated knights' armor and horses)

Tents of competitors

Heralds announce arrivals of knights

Musicians

Squires dressing knight for joust

Knight's helmet being removed

❸ Fatal fights

There were deaths at most tournaments, but some were worse than others. At a French tournament in 1240, many knights suffocated from heat and dust.

❺ "It's behind you!"

Both adults and children enjoyed the puppet shows that traveling players performed. The figures were glove puppets, and though the act resembled a Punch and Judy show, these characters did not appear until the 19th century.

❻ Playing knights

The winner of this piggyback-riding castle game was the "knight" who dismounted his opponent twice in three fights. The "horses" could shove with their shoulders but could not use their hands or feet.

❹ Lady's honor

Each knight fought for the honor of his lady and carried her favor into the joust. The favor was a token of her love, such as a sleeve or scarf, which the knight knotted around his lance.

❼ Bear baiting

Games that we consider cruel today were very popular. In bear baiting, people paid to watch their dogs fight a chained bear. If the bear yelped, the dog's owner won a cash prize.

❽ Hide the cat

There were no shops in the castle, so goods were bought from peddlers. Some peddlers were finely dressed merchants, but many were poor men who would catch stray cats to sell their fur if they thought no one was watching.

❾ Cockfighting

Roosters are very aggressive. An organized fight between two birds was called a "main." People often bet lots of money on which bird would kill the other.

❿ Alchemist at work

In primitive laboratories, alchemists tried to turn worthless metals into gold and to find an "elixir of life"—a medicine that cured all ills. Some experiments were magic, some fraud, and some a genuine search for scientific knowledge.

⓫ Hunting dogs

Hunting was an important part of castle life. The dogs lived in heated kennels, and ate special bread—brom bread—for their meals.

Guards playing dice

Women doing embroidery and playing instruments

Guard has lost all his clothes in a card game

Playing chess

Ferret kennels

Fortune-teller

Harvesting herbs

Children playing with tops

Wrestling match

Valiant knights

When noble boys were seven years old, they became pages and were taught how to behave in court and to practice good manners. This was the start of their knight training. The rules of chivalry applied to all soldiers, but to the knights most of all because they were warriors on horseback. The word chivalry comes from the French *chevalier*, meaning horseman.

Becoming a knight

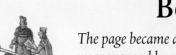

Lord dubbing a squire

The page became a squire, apprenticed to a knight, at 14 years old. Armor, weapons, and horses were expensive and the weapon training so tough that many squires did not achieve knight status at the age of 21. To make a young squire into a knight, the lord dubbed him. He struck a symbolic blow with the flat side of a sword or with his hand.

Chivalry

Knights had to obey a code of good conduct: a set of rules for gentlemen. The code, called chivalry, demanded that the knight should be brave, truthful, godly, gentle, faithful, and fearless. Chivalry also meant behaving honorably toward women. However, the laws of chivalry applied only to Christian nobles. They did not protect "heathens" (non-Christians) and villeins or other peasants.

Tapestry showing a nobleman giving a heart to a lady

Thou shalt be generous
The lord of the castle employed an almoner to distribute alms (charitable gifts) to the poor and needy. This was an essential part of chivalry. The more a lord gave, the faster he would go to heaven when he died.

Troubadours
Poet-musicians performed songs about love and chivalry during or after a feast. Called troubadours in France, they traveled from town to town. In a world where few people could read, they were also a good source of news and gossip.

Money could be given as alms, especially to the Church

Code of chivalry

1. Believe and observe all that the Church teaches.
2. Defend the Church.
3. Respect and defend all weaknesses.
4. Love the country of your birth.
5. Do not recoil before your enemy.
6. Make war against your enemy without cessation, and without mercy.
7. Perform your feudal duties scrupulously.
8. Never lie, and remain faithful to your pledged word.
9. Be generous to everyone.
10. Always be the champion of the Right and the Good against Injustice and Evil.

Heraldry

Armor made everyone look the same, so to avoid being killed by their own men, knights decorated their outfits with distinctive patterns called arms. The patterns became very elaborate, and there were complex rules, called heraldry, for their creation.

Merging arms

When families married, they merged their arms by dividing the shield. When their children married, it was divided again—and so on. This was called quartering, and by the 14th century, only heralds understood the complex system.

Wife's arms

Husband's arms

Lance measured about 13 ft (4m)

Herald

Well-off barons and knights employed one or more heralds to help them at the joust. A herald had many duties, but the most important at the joust was to act as a representative for his master.

| CROSS | DRAGON | LION RAMPANT | CHEVRON |

Heraldic charges

The shape of heraldic shields was based on the shields that knights used. The simplest shields were of one color, but many had systems of colors and a few featured crests.

Wearing arms

The knight's shield, painted with his arms, was held in the left arm to deflect the blow from the other knight's lance.

Equipment for the joust

Not much is known about 14th-century jousting equipment because most existing pieces date from later centuries. Early jousting helmets may have been slightly thicker to withstand the impact of an opponent's lance, with a reinforced plate below the eye slits. A long gauntlet (glove) called a manifer may also have been worn.

Even the horse wore the knight's colors

Reinforced helmet protected the face

Grand guard reinforced the left shoulder

Manifer protected the hand

Extra elbow defense, called a passegarde

Bottom left side protected by a tasset, which was strapped on

Drive on the right

Knights in the joust always passed to their opponent's left, so the left-hand side of the suit of armor was more heavily reinforced than the right. These armored pieces date from 1550 and show some of the reinforcements that knights wore.

Food supply

Supplying the castle with food was a major task. When the lord was at home, there were up to 200 hungry people to feed. Much of the food came from the manor—the land under control of the castle and its lord. The lord of the manor owned most of the land, but he allowed his subjects—the local people—to farm some of it. In exchange, they had to cultivate the lord's fields, called the demesne lands.

Armor needed constant polishing with animal fat to remove rust

❶ Firewood
Every castle needed fuel for cooking and heating. Villagers and servants collected firewood, making sure to take only dead or fallen timber. Any healthy wood was valuable as building material.

❷ Tools and carts
The castle blacksmith and carpenter made every tool and implement the castle needed. The tools and carts together were called "deadstock," to distinguish them from the animals—the livestock.

❸ Herbage
The grass that grew on the banks at the foot of the castle wall was not wasted. The pasture was called herbage. Villagers paid the lord a fee to graze their flocks there.

Fat of the land
Animal fat made tallow candles, prevented armor from rusting, and greased the wooden axles of carts and wagons.

Ale being delivered

You are here

This was the larder of the castle, where the livestock lived and where food was stored. Many castles were linked to a walled town by a fortified gate within a towered wall.

4 No dumping

The disposal of garbage was a problem in a castle. Much of it was tipped over the walls into a stinking heap in the castle ditch. Flies attracted to the dump caused health problems if the castle was near a town.

5 Salting meat

The most common way of preserving pork and beef through the winter was to salt it. The salt worked by locking up the water in the meat. The microorganisms that rot meat need water to live, so salt kept the meat from spoiling.

6 Slaughterhouse

A skilled butcher could kill a pig almost painlessly. He took care to make sure that the beast was happy right up to the moment when he hit its head with a hammer. This was common sense, not kindness—if the pig was scared, its meat was tougher.

7 Bee skeps

Honey was the only common sweetener, and the castle's bees lived in hives high on the walls. The hives, called skeps, were made of straw.

8 Mucking out

Oxen produced almost as much dung as they ate in food, and removing the muck was a full-time job.

9 Salt fish store

The castle kept a supply of salted fish called stockfish. Fish was very popular and was on the castle menu as often as meat.

10 Pigeon pie tonight

Collecting pigeons for the pot was easiest at night. Once the birds had roosted, the cook's assistants could lift them as easily as they could pick fruit from a tree.

Salt

Game birds (pheasants, partridges, woodcocks)

Corn, barley, and rye

43

Food, glorious food

The changing seasons controlled everyone's diet. In summer and autumn, there was plenty of fresh food. In winter, feed for animals was scarce, so the villagers slaughtered many of their pigs, sheep, poultry, and cattle at the end of autumn. To keep the meat from rotting, they preserved it in salt or by smoking. Other foods, such as beans, were preserved by drying. A few foodstuffs, such as apples, grew or could be stored until spring.

Livestock

In medieval times, farm animals, such as sheep, cattle, and pigs, were smaller and thinner than today's animals. They took a long time to grow to a size that was suitable for eating, so they lived longer than animals today. Poorer people tended to keep birds such as chickens and geese that provided eggs as well as meat.

SHEARS

Sheep
The sheep that grazed on the lord's lands were a valuable asset. Their wool was sold to make cloth. Shearing the sheep produced matted fleeces of wool that fetched a high price abroad. The wool trade was important to England for hundreds of years.

Chickens
Nobles ate chicken frequently. For poorer households, eggs were more important, so these birds were eaten only on special occasions and usually when they no longer laid eggs.

Cattle
During the winter, when grass grew slowly, cows had to eat hay from the stack. They had huge appetites, so most castles kept only enough cows for breeding in the spring. A few castles, however, kept extra cattle for milking.

Beasts for feasts

Within the lord's lands were beasts that were caught and eaten only on special occasions. Some of these animals were a display of wealth when strutting around the grounds. Deer were hunted for feasts, and a stag, called a hart, was a real prize. Some lords enclosed parts of forests so that the deer could be caught more easily.

Acorn feast
Pigs cost almost nothing to keep because they didn't need to be fed but scratched for food in the forest. However, feeding acorns to hogs fattened them up nicely, and roast boar was a favorite dish for the lord at Christmas.

Pricey peacock
The wealthiest barons kept peacocks and swans to decorate their castle grounds and to eat. A favorite banquet dish was roast peacock. In a true show of wealth, its feet would sometimes be brushed with powdered gold.

BEER BARREL

WINE TASTER

Brewing

Wine was generally kept for special occasions and Sundays, and was the drink of nobility. Ale was far more common and less expensive than wine, and was the drink of choice for the majority of people. It was sometimes mixed with spices, brandy, or milk, but no matter how it came, huge quantities of ale were drunk by the population.

ALE CONNER

More ale!

Ale did not keep well, so brewing went on all the time. The castle brewed some of its own ale but also bought barrels of ale in the market. To satisfy the thirsty occupants of the largest castles, the carter hauled wagonloads of ale through the castle gates.

The ale conner

Testing the purity of beer was the job of the ale conner. He poured a pool of ale onto a wooden bench and then sat in it. The ale passed the test if his leather britches were not stuck to the bench after half an hour. Poor-quality beer was sugary and would glue him to the seat. The punishment for producing low-quality beer was probably the pillory.

Boon day

At harvest time, the lord called a "boon day," and every able-bodied person had to help with cutting, turning, and stacking the hay. Cutting the hay and grain was very hard work but had its rewards: The villagers were given a large meal and often all the ale they could drink. At the day's end, there were amusing harvest traditions. A sheep was released into the stubble and the villagers could keep it if it stayed in the field. If it strayed, the lord reclaimed the beast.

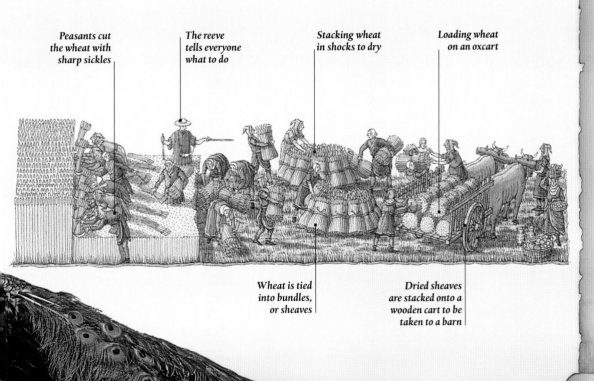

Peasants cut the wheat with sharp sickles

The reeve tells everyone what to do

Stacking wheat in shocks to dry

Loading wheat on an oxcart

Wheat is tied into bundles, or sheaves

Dried sheaves are stacked onto a wooden cart to be taken to a barn

Tax demand

The lord charged a bewildering array of fees and taxes. Here are some examples:

 Wood-penny: for the right to collect firewood

 Agistment: for the right to graze animals in the forest

 Chiminage: for the right to carry goods through the forest

 Bodel silver: for the right to live in a house on the lord's land

 Foddercorn: grain a villein had to provide to feed the lord's horses

 Heriot: upon death, a family had to give the lord the dead man's best animal

Lawbreakers

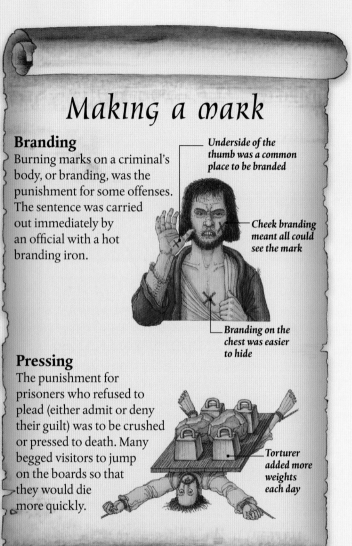

Making a mark

Branding
Burning marks on a criminal's body, or branding, was the punishment for some offenses. The sentence was carried out immediately by an official with a hot branding iron.

Underside of the thumb was a common place to be branded

Cheek branding meant all could see the mark

Branding on the chest was easier to hide

Pressing
The punishment for prisoners who refused to plead (either admit or deny their guilt) was to be crushed or pressed to death. Many begged visitors to jump on the boards so that they would die more quickly.

Torturer added more weights each day

Castles that protected towns often had a second entrance. This "town gate" was a handy way in and out of the castle. Grisly sights greeted the traders and troops who passed through the gate. Staring down from pikes high on the walls were the heads of executed traitors. In the ditch stood the gallows and pillory. Like the severed heads above, they reminded people of the punishments for breaking the law.

Bagpipes are played to humiliate the offender

You are here

The garrison stored the siege weapons and their ammunition in the arsenal tower. The trebuchet had to be taken apart in order to fit inside the castle.

Store of small stones for hand throwing at the enemy

❶ Gallows

Execution by hanging (strangulation with a rope) on the gallows (the frame from which the rope hung) was the penalty for serious crime. It was a slow death, and many victims begged their friends to hasten death by pulling on their legs.

❷ Drawing

For treason (plotting against the king), prisoners were "hung, drawn, and quartered." The half-dead victim was taken off the gallows, and his insides were cut out. The hangman held up the victim's heart and shouted, "Behold the heart of a traitor!"

❸ Quartering

The final stage of a traitor's fate was to be quartered: chopped into four pieces. The quarters, or sometimes just the head, were put on public display.

❹ Duck!

Another punishment was ducking in the moat. The offender was seated in a "ducking stool" and lowered into the water.

❺ Pillory

For minor crimes, such as selling underweight goods, there was the pillory. This wooden structure had holes to grip the offender's head and hands. For slightly more serious offenses, such as spreading false rumors, the prisoner's ears were nailed back to the boards.

❻ Hanging in chains

For particularly unfortunate criminals, punishment didn't end on the gallows. The blacksmith riveted the corpse into "chains"—an iron framework—and the body was displayed hanging from a gibbet (beam) to warn others against crime.

❼ Getting ahead

The heads of traitors decorated the castle battlements above the gates as a warning to others who plotted against the king. There they were lightly boiled before being dipped in preservative tar. The heads looked out over other public places, too, such as the entrances to bridges.

❽ Drawbridge pit

The drawbridge dropped into a deep pit as it closed. In its open position, the drawbridge sealed the pit, which made a useful extra punishment cell. A few drawbridges were booby trapped to release a trapdoor that pitched unwanted visitors into the pit.

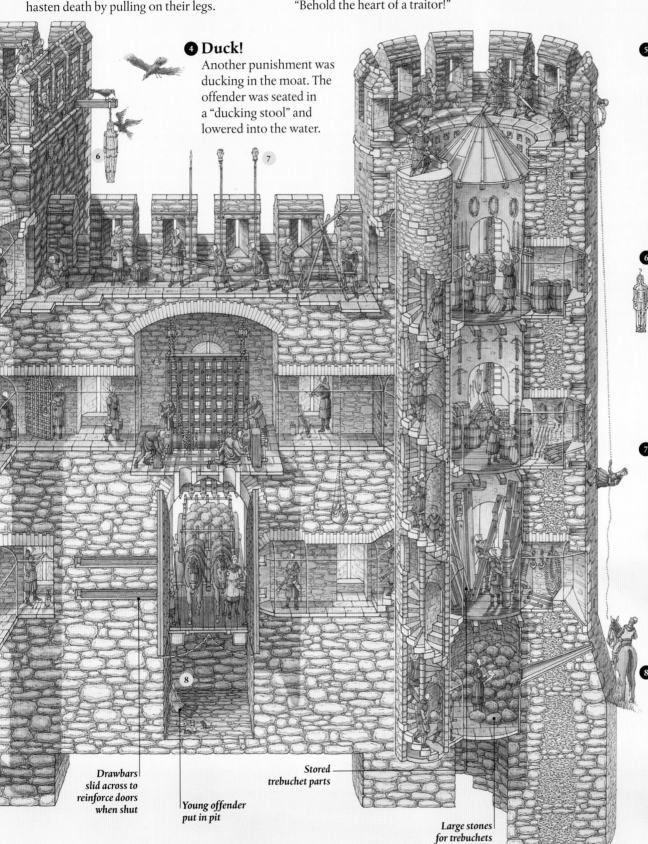

Drawbars slid across to reinforce doors when shut

Young offender put in pit

Stored trebuchet parts

Large stones for trebuchets

Weaponry

I n the shadow of the town gate were the butts. These were targets where every able-bodied man had to practice his archery skills each week. Preparations for warfare took place inside the castle walls, too. When they weren't rehearsing their fighting skills, the members of the castle garrison were busy laying in stores and ammunition, or repairing their weapons.

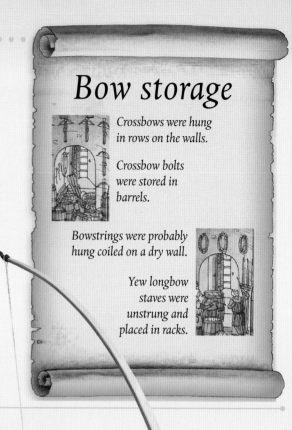

Bow storage

Crossbows were hung in rows on the walls.

Crossbow bolts were stored in barrels.

Bowstrings were probably hung coiled on a dry wall.

Yew longbow staves were unstrung and placed in racks.

Practicing marksmanship

Training in archery started in boyhood, with a small bow and a nearby target. However, men had to stand more than 722 ft (220 m) from the target, and use much more powerful bows. Instead of the sharp, armor-piercing points used in warfare, practice arrows had blunt tips.

CROSSBOWMAN

Cord drawn back ready to fire the bolt

LONGBOWMAN

Yew was favorite wood for longbow

Bowstring usually made of hemp or flax

Crossbow
The crossbow was a powerful weapon. To help the crossbow arrow, or bolt, pierce armor plating, the bowman put a glob of beeswax on the tip. If the bolt struck the armor at an angle, the wax helped the tip grip the plating and penetrate it.

Arrows made of ash wood

CROSSBOW

Release nut

Windlass drew back bowstring

Barbs on head caused nasty wounds

Longbow
The longbow required great skill to fire accurately. However, in the hands of a good archer, the longbow was powerful enough to put an arrow through an oak panel. It was also quick to fire. A longbowman could fire four arrows while a crossbowman was still loading.

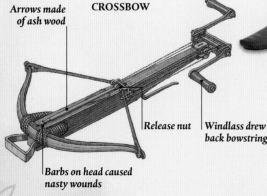

Throwing power

The only war engine that could be operated from the top of a castle tower was the mangonel. Using a trebuchet on a tower would shake it to pieces. Instead, trebuchets were dismantled and stored in parts in the arsenal tower. When needed for a siege on another lord's castle, the huge trebuchets were loaded onto carts and assembled within range of the rival castle's walls.

Mangonel

The range of a mangonel was about 1,300 ft (400 m). A windlass (winch) turned and tightened a twisted rope that held a long wooden arm in firing position. A large cup at the end of the arm held ammunition. When the windlass was released, the force of the rope untwisting propelled the arm forward until it hit a crossbeam, shooting ammunition out of the cup toward its target.

Cup for ammunition

Crossbeam

Twisted rope

Ammunition

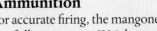
For accurate firing, the mangonel needed carefully cut stones. Weight was important, because a stone that was too light would travel beyond the target, while stones that were too heavy fell short.

Hammer — Spike

Ax

Cut and crush

Crossbows were the most useful weapons in the castle, but when the enemy approached too near, other weapons were employed. The type of weapon used by a soldier depended on whether he was on foot or on horseback, and whether he was wearing armor.

Poleax

A foot soldier used long, two-handed poleaxes against a knight's head. A poleax had three means of attack: the spike was thrust into the opponent, the hammer crushed the body, and the ax cut through armor.

Great sword

The most distinguished weapon, the sword was used by a knight to cut through an opponent's chain mail. The narrow, sharp point was thrust between armored plates.

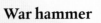
Sword was swung with both hands for a powerful blow

Hammer

Pick

War hammer

Men-at-arms on horseback used war hammers to smash armored knights with heavy blows. The pick pierced armor and the hammer stunned the knight.

Glossary

arrow loops
Narrow slits in castle walls used for firing arrows.

ashlar
Building stone that is trimmed to shape.

atilliator
A skilled castle worker who made crossbows.

bailey
An open area enclosed by castle walls.

battlements
Jagged stonework that protected the wall-walk.

boon day
A compulsory workday when manor workers helped in the lord's fields.

buttery
The room where wine was dispensed from barrels.

butts
Targets for town archery practice.

chivalry
Rules of polite and honorable behavior that knights were supposed to follow.

constable
A person who took care of a castle when the owner was away.

crenellations
Jagged protective stonework at the top of the castle wall.

crenels
Low sections of the battlements.

daub
A mud coating—much like plaster—smeared on wattle.

embrasures
Arrow loops in the merlons.

ewerer
A worker who brought and heated water for the knight and his family to wash in.

garrison
A group of soldiers guarding the castle.

herald
A knight's assistant, representative at the joust, and expert advisor on heraldry.

heraldry
The rules controlling the use by noblemen of the distinctive patterns used on their flags, armor, and shields.

hoarding
A defensive wooden extension of the castle wall-walk.

hoarding holes
Holes in the castle walls to support the hoarding.

jousting
A knight's war game played on horseback. Armored opponents charged at each other, each using his lance to knock the other from the saddle.

keep
A fortified tower containing living quarters, situated at the heart of the castle.

lance
A long, pointed pole used as a weapon in war and jousting.

mangonel
A siege engine that used the power in a twisted cord to fire missiles.

merlons
High sections of the battlements.

moat
A water-filled ditch around the castle.

murder holes
Holes in the floor that allowed archers to fire into the room below.

oubliette
A tiny cell where prisoners were left to die.

pillory
A punishment frame that usually gripped a victim's hands and head while onlookers threw garbage.

portcullis
A sliding grid of stout wood used to guard the castle entrance.

quarrel
An arrow for a crossbow.

quintain
A target for jousting practice.

siege
The surrounding of a castle to cut off its supplies and make the occupants surrender.

siege engine
A machine for firing missiles at a castle, or for scaling walls.

squire
A young trainee knight who served as an assistant to an older knight.

tournament
A knight's war-game that imitated real battles; often used to mean jousting.

trebuchet
A giant siege engine in the form of a boulder-firing catapult.

troubadour
A professional musician who usually traveled from town to town.

turning bridge
A drawbridge that is pivoted in the middle.

villein
A common laborer living on a knight's estate in near slavery.

wall-walk
A footpath around the top of the castle walls.

wattle
A woven panel of twigs used in building.

Arrow loops

Jousting

Mangonel

Pillory

Trebuchet   *Wattle and daub*

Index

A
alchemist 39
ale 27, 45
alms 40
animal fat 42
animals 31, 38, 39, 44, 45
apprentices 26, 28
archery 25, 48
archive 23, 31
armor 21, 27, 29, 41, 42
arms, heraldic 41
arrow loops 25
arrows, flaming 13, 17, 23
arsenal tower 46–47
ashlar 25
atilliator 27
attacks 11, 12, 13, 14–17

B
bailey 10–11
barons 20
basket boys 22
bathing 35
battering ram 17
bear baiting 39
bed 30
bee skeps 43
belfry 17
betrothal ceremony 31, 32
blacksmith 24, 42
bloodletting 30
boar 38, 44
Bodiam Castle 11
books 33
boon day 45
boots 29
branding 46
bread 35
brewing 27, 45
building 24–25
buttery 35
butts 48

C
candles 27, 42
carpenter 24, 42
carts 42
"cat" device 17
cats 31, 39
cattle 44
chain mail 29
chapel 30, 31, 33
chaplain 31, 33
Chepstow Castle 10
chickens 44
children 32, 39
Chinon Castle 10
chivalry 40
clothing 28–29, 32
cockfighting 39
constable 18, 19
court rolls 23
craftsmen 22, 24, 26–27
cranes 23
crenellations 21
crenels 12, 13
crime 23, 31, 46–47
crossbows 15, 17, 25, 27, 48
cutlery 35

D
deer 44
defenses 11, 12–13, 15
demesne lands 42
ditch clearing 26
doctor 30, 33
dogs 38, 39
drawbridge 10, 13
drawbridge pit 47
ducking stool 47
dungeons 19
dyeing 27, 28

E
early castles 10
education 31, 32, 33
eel traps 35
embrasures 13
entertainment 37, 38–39
executions 46–47

F
farming 42, 44–45
feasts 34–35, 37, 44
feudalism 20–21
fire 13, 23
firepots 17
firewood 42, 45
fish 34, 35, 43
flag 27
food 14, 15, 34–37, 42–45
food taster 35
fool 11, 37
freemen 20
freestone 25

G
gallery 30
gallows 46, 47
games 39
garbage 43
gardens 38
garrison 18–19, 46–47
gatehouse 10, 11, 12–13, 18–19
gauntlets 21, 29, 41
glass 30
gong farmer 11, 19
grappling iron 17
great hall 30, 34–35, 37
guards 13, 21, 39

H
hanging 47
harvest 45
hawking 38
heads, severed 46, 47
helmets 21, 41
heraldry 41
herbage 42
herbs 33, 36, 37, 39
hoardings 13, 15
homage 21
honey 43
hunting 38, 39, 44

J
Jamille Castle 21
jester 37
jousting 30, 38–39, 41

K
keep 10, 26–27, 30
king 20
kitchens 36

knights
knights 11, 14, 20, 29, 38–39, 40–41, 49

L
ladies-in-waiting 33
lady of the manor 32
lady's honor 39
lances 38, 40–41
larder 42–43
latrines 11, 12, 18, 19
law
  judge and jury 23
  punishment 46–47
lead 22, 23, 26
leather 29
  making bate for 23
licence to crenellate 21
limewash 26
livestock 44, 45
longbows 25, 48
lookout 19
lord 20, 23, 24, 27, 30–31, 32, 40, 42
  family 11, 32–33

M
machicolation 17
mangonel 16, 49
manor 42
marriage 32, 41
meat 36, 43, 44
merchants 29, 39
merlons 13
metal 24
  lead 22, 23, 26
minstrels 37
missiles 17
moat 10, 11, 13, 14, 30, 34
mortar 22
motte-and-bailey 10
mucking out 43
multure 27
murder holes 15
musicians 37, 38, 40

NO
nails 24
oubliette 19

P
pages 11, 33, 40
palisade 10
parapets 11
peacocks 44
peasants 20, 29, 35, 36, 45
peddlers 39
peepholes 19
pigeons 43
pigs 43, 44
pillory 46, 47
plumber 26
poleax 49
portcullis 12, 19
possessions 33
potter 27
pressing 46
priest 11, 33
prisoners 18, 19, 46, 47
punishments 46–47
puppet shows 39
putlog holes 15, 22

QR
quarrels (arrows) 15
quintain 30
reeve 45
repairs 22–23
roofing 13, 22, 23

S
sally port 17
salt 37, 43
sappers 16, 17
scaffolding 22
seating 35
servants 32, 33, 34, 36
sewage 30
shaving 34
sheep 44
shields 41
shingles 23
sieges 14, 15, 16–17, 22, 23, 49
silver plate 33
slaughterhouse 43
sluices 35
solar 30, 31
spices 31, 37
spinning 27, 28
spitting 37

sports
sports 38
squint 19
squires 33, 40
stone 10, 22, 25
stonemasons 22, 24, 25
supplies 14, 42–43
swords 49

T
tailors 27, 29
tapestries 32–33, 35, 40
taxes 23, 31, 45
thatch 23
tools 24, 42
torture 31, 46
towers 10–11, 12–13, 46–47
town gate 46
traitors 46, 47
treadmill 23
treasury 31
trebuchet 15, 16, 46, 47, 49
trencher 36
troubadours 37, 40

VW
vaulted ceiling 31
villeins 20, 45
walls 10–11, 12, 23, 25
  limewash 26
war hammer 49
watchmen 12, 13
watchtower 10–11, 13
water 23, 24, 31
wattle and daub 23, 25
weapons 15, 16, 17, 21, 25, 48–49
  jousting 38, 40–41
well 23, 31
winch room 19
windmill 27
windows 30
wine 34, 35, 36, 45
women 27, 28, 39
wood 14, 24, 26, 42
wool 28, 29, 44
workers 26–27, 32, 33

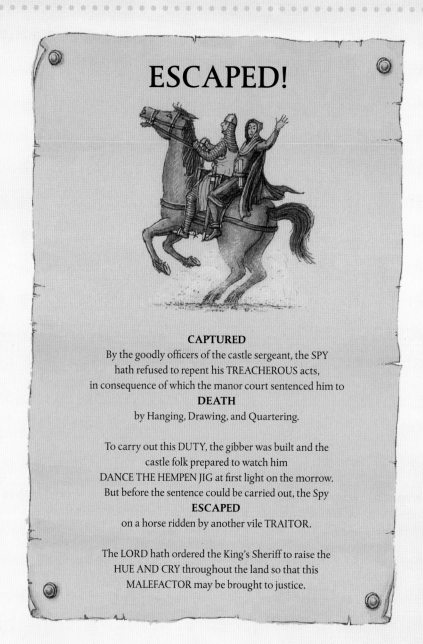

ESCAPED!

CAPTURED
By the goodly officers of the castle sergeant, the SPY
hath refused to repent his TREACHEROUS acts,
in consequence of which the manor court sentenced him to
DEATH
by Hanging, Drawing, and Quartering.

To carry out this DUTY, the gibber was built and the
castle folk prepared to watch him
DANCE THE HEMPEN JIG at first light on the morrow.
But before the sentence could be carried out, the Spy
ESCAPED
on a horse ridden by another vile TRAITOR.

The LORD hath ordered the King's Sheriff to raise the
HUE AND CRY throughout the land so that this
MALEFACTOR may be brought to justice.

Acknowledgments

DK would like to thank:
Ashwin Khurana for additional editorial work,
Fran Jones for proofreading, and Jackie Brind
for preparing the index.

**The publisher would like to thank the
following for their kind permission
to reproduce their photographs:**

Key: a=above; b=below; c=center; f =far;
l =left; t = top

**The Bodleian Library, University of
Oxford**: 37cb. **Dorling Kindersley**: The
American Museum of Natural History 16tr,
16ftr; Anthony Barton Collection 37clb,
37fbl; The Trustees of the British Museum
27br, 40clb, 40cb (l), 40cb (r), 40bc; Dean and
Chapter of Canterbury Cathedral 30cla, 30cl;
Torla Evans / Museum of London 24clb, 36fcrb
(jar); Gordon Models - modelmaker 10c; Musee
National du Moyen-Age Thermes de Cluny
40fclb; National Guild of Stone Masons and
Carvers, London 24cl; National Maritime
Museum, London 46ftr; Order of the Black
Prince 28cr; Board of Trustees of the Royal
Armouries 15fcla; The Science Museum,
London 14br; The Silver Fund / Judith Miller
34cla; Wallace Collection, London 40ftl,
41crb, 49c, 49crb, 49br; Whitbread PLC 45ftl.

Dreamstime.com: Vadim Yerofeyev 6fbl,
7fbr, 8fbl, 9fbr, 10fbl, 11fbr, 12fbl, 13fbr, 14fbl,
15fbr, 16fbl, 17fbr, 18fbl, 19fbr, 20fbl, 21fbr,
22fbl, 23fbr, 24fbl, 25fbr, 26fbl, 27fbr, 28fbl,
29fbr, 30fbl, 31fbr, 32fbl, 33fbr, 34fbl, 35fbr,
36fbl, 37fbr, 38fbl, 39fbr, 40fbl, 41fbr, 42fbl,
43fbr, 44fbl, 45fbr, 46fbl, 47fbr, 48fbl, 49fbr,
50fbl, 51fbr, 52fbl.

All other images © Dorling Kindersley
For further information see:
www.dkimages.com